Could be

Also by Heather Cadsby

Traditions
Decoys
A Tantrum of Synonyms

Could be

Poems by Heather Cadsby

Brick Books

Library and Archives Canada Cataloguing in Publication

Cadsby, Heather
     Could be / Heather Cadsby.

Poems.
ISBN 978-1-894078-73-3

I. Title.

PS8555.A27C347 2009   C811'.54   C2009-902315-6

We acknowledge the Canada Council for the Arts, the Government
of Canada through the Book Publishing Industry Development
Program (BPIDP), and the Ontario Arts Council for their support
of our publishing program.

Cover art: excerpts from *History Painting Project* by Mark Bell,
watercolour on Bristol paper; on-going since 2002.

The author photograph was taken by Alison Hancock.

The book is set in Minion and Helvetica.

Design and layout by Alan Siu.

Printed and bound by Sunville Printco Inc.

Brick Books
431 Boler Road, Box 20081
London, Ontario N6K 4G6

www.brickbooks.ca

For

Maculloch Edward Bell

Sadie Ila Bell

Jodie Yvonne Cadsby

Mackenzie Clarissa Cadsby

Contents

House Party

An ornithologist ran through here
while you were in the washroom. You missed it.
He was in costume. Actually he looked like me.
Only way taller. And he was black.

A blackbird just flew through here
while you were getting another drink.
You missed it of course.
She was dragging a ukulele by its g-string.
It moved so smoothly along the floor
I thought it was something else
for a moment. The ukulele that is.
The bird was ordinary, much like myself.
And, come to think of it, you.
Except you are way smaller and much redder
than any birdface. What's new in the kitchen?
You really should go and fix yourself.
We've missed so much already.

Ironies, similes, not exactly

You can get it if you calm down
and embalm the ambiguities. The first few on the list
are easy to hammer into your head. In fact
I'd skip the first two, *Maybe this, maybe that.*

I should get my ears checked. That's not
the way you heard it. No, no
it wasn't ear wax. It was earwigs
that weaselled their way under the sill.
But this is what makes it so interesting. Like
when he said the pattern on his flipflops
was the same as on the vanilla wafers.
It was very exciting to hear and to be honest
that was when I fell for his cryptic ways.

So the next ambiguity would be *Pick up your stuff.*
Or maybe not. At any rate
the next to last is *Your troubles are over.*
Music to my ears even though the curtain
on the left was hanging below the sill
and I'd already paid. I really did want to believe him.
Who remembers these things?

Are we this far already? *You can come along
if you want to.* That old scene
you once wanted to know about, but not more than
you needed to know what want meant.
And *All the promise in the world* (well down on the list)
didn't produce a picture to me.
If the doors are locked
how important are your secrets anyway?

Simply put, this is all about me and others.
Bye dear. The music is fine. Just keep hearing,
and faith in your afterthoughts.

Aubade

Praise be to the angels of morning breath.
A waft of nasty odour is a sign of life.
Praise a stretch, a crusty eyelid,
stars in the skylight and light in the sky.
I am a woman. I am a man. Praise that.
Praise new formalism, old jewellery,
a friend's negligence and certain choreography.
Praise a missed step at first light,
a twisted ankle, big awkward feet,
the application of witch hazel
and the promise of pancakes.
Praise sudden fear at daybreak,
the body returned to thought.

Floating double, swan and shadow (Wordsworth), as the planet heads into

A poem in 5 parts

The music (Sibelius)
The painting (Delacroix)
Folktale imprints science
The ballet (Swan Lake)
Seasonal inventory

The music (Sibelius)

Saw 12 swans at 10 to 11 this morning: his journal.
Was he looking straight ahead or over his shoulder?

Were they V-flying or countable on the river?
What did he hear and how was the light settling

on this fatherless son who composed
with an eye to the past? Were the bills

orange or black? But look. This is nonsense.
We have the *Swan of Tuonela*.

Songs of the land. Huge white swimming birds.
Expensive cognac. But not before noon.

The painting (Delacroix)

To render glimpses of nature
is to contemplate shackled ankles.

I paint stopped short, yanked
and disabled. So swans are displaced

and reproduced with Turkish women bathing
not for adornment or subject matter. I do not

need more soft curved items. I give you women
to do with as you wish. The swans

are untransferable.
Could snap off a dog's leg.

Folktale imprints science

A mother-to-be has fixed dreams
says, "I'll love it whatever."

Near the end gets impatient
says, "I feel pretty awful."

And if the lastborn is bigger
or greyer or has a long neck,

a small reluctance is also present.
To be graceful as a swan, is not

to be a duck. To be *trumpeter*
is not to be *mute*. Even if wildfowl

experts remove you gently, paint your black bill
orange, and tuck you back under as a perfect match,

who is saved
as a bill grows soft?

The ballet (Swan Lake)

The (swan) bird resplendent in her 25,000 feathers
soars like a cross (northern), plummets if

more than 4 outer ones (pennae) are disabled. The (swan) dancer
needs 2 arms to flutter through 3 hours (deduct intermissions) to sustain

the illusion that once she soared and even in a plummeted state
she can rivet (grand jetés). A (swan) bird can still fall

from the sky, feathers intact, but gunshot. We love
our down. It's cozy here in the mezzanine with all this whiteness

and smoke coming in from the wings. I can't believe
in that redhead. I like my (swan) girls dark-haired

under the headpiece. Can the director
fire her?

Seasonal inventory

Here is the end: the secret is a bird
growing by story and image.

The wings may be affixed with wax
but the preen gland supplies the oil.

The boy's bones need to lighten,
to become pneumatic. This takes time.

Prison designers brush eraser crumbs
from first drafts. What is rubber?

Tankers clean their bilges. What is oil?
What is plastic? Leg rings for census,

for hybrids, for the new taxonomy. Turns out
the orange-dyed bills may not be *that* soft.

Either/Or unplugged

Are you an artist if you only draw horses?
If all you want to be is a jockey
but you are a big person and even riding
off into the sunset is wishful because
you are a big smoker among big smokers
and an early autumn sunset is in part man-made.
Man, I made that. Hand me those pastels, will you.

Are you a poet if you only submit once in a while?
And all you want to be is somebody's girlfriend
but you are a grandmother by some miracle
and M=A=M=I=E is mostly vowels. And M starts with E.
You say, I could have written that book myself. I am
a recipient of arts grants, get invitations to read and lecture
all from a very high horse.

Any questions?

Are you very high standing atop two horses
whip-cracking your way around Ricoh Coliseum?
         A Texas trick rider needs screaming children.

Are you very high riding your police horse doing crowd control?
         There are crying children at ground level.

Where is the higher ground on a high road of highest order?
         Everything all at once.

Time for one more.

Is the sketch of a poetry question? Cut.

Bridge over Mimico Creek

A boy was throwing pieces of bread
at the ducks. I said, "Excuse me but
that is killing them." He turned and
said, "Lady, these ain't stones."
The confusion was clear. I cleared
my throat and he spit on the ground.
It seemed he wanted to share. The mallards
clearly loved him and his bag of bread.
"It's fuckin whole grain," he said.
I said, "OK," and put my hand out.
"But I don't really believe in feeding
wild things. I think it disturbs."
"Hey they love it," he said.
And I could see how I wanted to be fooled.
"If I had a gun," he said. I could see how
I could be fooled. "You look pretty angry,"
I said. "Whadaya want from me," he said.
I could see I was fooling myself
and making a fool of myself. I bit
my tongue, let out a yelp and
took off in a huff.

In regard to No

No carries something that feels like it's not coming back.
Our worst fear. Whether body intact or love.
Firmly shouted, it carries itself like a question.
It has no mind.
No thought made word.
What precedes the spoken No
has been packed and unpacked and rehashed.

No carries something that feels like preview to regret.
The Little Red Hen thing. Her bad friends.
Not I. Not I. Not I.
Oh, I wish I'd said yes.

The bullysong. NO. You can't have
your lunch back
your jacket back
your courage back
your sex back
your belief back

Always the imbricated imbroglios.

Do you believe in God? No.
Do you believe in God? Who are you?
I'm yours.
We'll see.

One longs for No from a more reliable source.

Speaking of No, the strongest case would be amen.

Sorry to say

The Party Rentals truck has flipped over
into the condo tulip bed. The gardening
committee is mostly scattered.
I myself was just heading out. The tow truck
is blocking the garage exit. I had to drive back to my spot
and return to my unit. The good thing is
I can watch all this from my window. And I can
make myself a coffee. There's always a silver lining
even when someone's party is in shambles. I hope
it's that nasty woman upstairs who was planning
a birthday for herself. Probably broken china,
bent cutlery and wonky chairs in that truck now.
This is very exciting. Think I'll have another coffee.

Someone has given coffee to the two drivers
and they've started yelling.
"Whadayamean thirty eighty-five!
This place is forty. Yah, forty eighty-five."

This is no good. I can't get excited about
imagining a nasty person in some other building.

One way or another

Descend upon Me
O muse of startling dog bark,
3 a.m. shouts and shots,
fatherly beatings, sorrowful virgins,
inducements to art. O giver of content
hit Me.

O muse of the mellow mist season,
long shadow of yellow-leafed tree,
drawn-out train whistle,
wasps harvesting cider or pear,
soccer field of pumpkins.
You current of the songs of autumn
stroll into my art form.

O triangulate Courted One
of the Beckett jokes and diminishings
of the perhaps and wandering Ashbery
of the sonnetful Raymond Queneau
hit on Me.

O Bigwig of quirky wordthings
you chapped-lipped second-order angel,
ripper of old nails and rotten thresholds,
smash through this.
Land on and muse Me.

Would you like to have a poem, I know I would

She phones. Says she's written a new poem and wants my comments.
"Sure," I say, "get your ass over here and bring some wine." That's
how we always talk when one of us has a new boyfriend. "You bet,"
she says, "and while I'm on my way, please give some thought to stinky
feet." Oh boy, I think to myself, that could be real trouble. And by the
time she buzzes my apartment I am in a sweat. "Hey Hi Hello pal," she
says all cheery and pours some wine. "Pinot," she says. "But this is
white," I say. "Different version," she says. Pretty watery, I think to
myself. Then I say, "So about your title, Stinky Feet, I have problems
with it." "Yeah, knew you'd say that. Do I know you or what! Lemme
explain. On the surface it's about this guy who gets kicked out of
Greenpeace. So it works on that level. Then you have the Cinderella
and dry cleaning references in the third stanza. So that works." "Wait,
wait, wait," I say. "So that water/wine thing is a trope?" "A what?"
"A metaphor." "Oh my god, have I wrecked this? The Jesus stuff was
supposed to be obscure." "Well," I say, "there are feet in the title and
that, I feel, is a problem. My suggestion is..." "Oh geez," she says,
"let me leave this with you. I don't want to be late for the third date."
So, to be kind, I say, "Feet can be sexy." Not dispirited, just protective
of my own.

Aubade

At first light
a veery's tumbling song
and everything I knew was feared.
The sun took root
and I thought if I could just lie down in a field
I would understand my life
and the falling away of death – yours
and also the three infant losses.
But I could not lie upon the ground.
There was a solemn child
sitting on the stairs.
Birds spread across the sky like silence
on a face scored for silence.

Single woman on the death of her mother

1

I grew impatient with waiting
as my mother was dying.
I stood rigid in elevators, a potential griever
who allowed her mother to pull off the oxygen mask,
by leaving the room, going down for coffee.
And on returning, snapped the thing
back into place as the mother winced.
Who did I think I guarded.

I grew mean with waiting
as my mother was dying.
She wasn't answering, seemed to be sleeping.
I looked for stale-dating on the IV bag.
I banged my leg into her bed,
forced bad breath out of my mouth.
I grabbed her thumb
and was just about to yell mommy
when she opened her eyes and was gone.

2

And so the question where are you now.
Where is here and there
in a space that has escaped the confines of my world.
Here you are disruptive. There you are futural.
Not a memory yet
just a dispersion of what sheltered and disturbed.

A few days after your death
I awoke from a nap with a feeling
that something was lifting from my chest
or a lightness was lifting me.

3

You gave me life.
What did you have in mind?

You gave me life.
What is lost?

You gave me life.
Nothing is taken away.

Give me rage.
Not this dull dumb torpor,
this weary body moving down the aisle of pet foods.
I have no cat, no dog, no bird.
Let me shake the shelves of canned goods
till they spew and crash on all of us
and I will be hit with
the strength to believe I am now alone.

Jabberwocky, you read to me.
What a lovely way to pass the time.
Here, now, there, when.
Praise for the vorpal sword: a voice raised in vocables.

The phonic and the graphic.
I direct my voice to say mother.
I have Helen carved on the stone.
You are neither unified nor authentic in this.

What is witnessed in a signature
is a living hand. Once.
I don't have that luxury now.

Where are you now that I've given everything away?
I take for mine your death
and this path I'm on
and going on through.

Something occurs before thought.
Before *I must tell mother that oh no I can't.*
Something comes and leaves so quickly it drags no emotion.
I came from your body. It might come from that.
It might be the growth of death.
Certainly something is trying to work its way up.

If it's too private, it's unreliable.
What did you say? What did I remember?
You said your grandfather said,
"Child, child, what will become of the parsonage furniture."
Who cares about that anymore than you did
jumping and bouncing in 1910.

As long as you were alive
I could speak with you.
Now I speak about you.

As long as you were alive
I thought I had the whole story:
my grievances and your angry laugh.
It seemed an absolute fidelity
between two daily lives.
Now I need someone else to die
so I can deserve all this grief.

Recursus

The philosopher on the footbridge said
if you are sad you believe in sadness.

The birds are not flying.
On this day of all days if you see
a common pintail among the mallards it is rare.

A siren is wailing.
And in this city of all cities if another black boy has been shot
the white men will be saying my son.

The church bells are clanging.
If you are a closed mouth singing
you are nearer to tears. If I say I believe
I am not a believer. Mimico Creek is sparkling
on this morning of all mornings. I say it is enough
to make me a believer. It is a clear sign.

O self
is just another sign.
Behold on the west bank
two friends seemingly.
Let's say happily.

The truth is always a bit further on

Someone sneezed. We'd been
throwing around the question of collections.
She'd said horse brass or cobalt eyecups.
By the time we mentioned you
we were indifferent. But then
someone said you'd received a grant
for your feather project. Allergies notwithstanding.
We remembered your grandfather
had taken away the pillow. Snufflenose
or whatever was said in those days. Turns out
the granting folks fell for your curriculum vitae.
She thought it was the back, left, right sleep pattern
that did it. I was more convinced
by your favourite isotope. But apparently
you'd added the intention of a new fridge
for safe storage.

So there it was. An attempt to prove
that birds of a feather flock together
and you needed a collection. Or rather
a larger one. We'd all been bored to death
with that box of found and plucked.
Idiot, your father said. Thinks he's
looking for fingerprints.
Well sort of, you'd said. It's
more like signatures.
And on and on about
bits of DNA that stick.
I said, sebum.
She said, sexy. Why doesn't he
collect pubic hair?
It was only later we became curious
about the polymorphic sparrow.

One school of thought

If you've got the high notes
you might as well show them off.
Well, in a provisional way.
You wouldn't want to let it rip
out there on the curb
in the face of trash collectors
who are halfway through a day of sorting
and halfway pissed off already
and not about to applaud a boy soprano.

You can do it at home for the family.
But that has its own trade-offs.
You have to play goalie on the driveway
and scapegoat in the underwear game.

But look, as one who has spent
years counter-tenoring, I say
go for it. Shatter the chandelier
with chaos and colour. Hell,
demolish the whole block.
Caruso the suburb. Belt it out.
Hold that high C. Tremolo tremolo.
God-love-us Tiny Tim.

Just about all we're about

Will you look at that tree?
It hasn't caught up to its dying.

There are green leaves among the yellow ones.
It looks like a banana tree in this light.

Empty branches lead the story for next year.
Last year we paid to have it pruned.

I said no to chemo.
This tree just took it on the chin.

You said goldfinch, not canary.
It's true about detection. But where?

Ah well, we can swim here
near the tree

or over there in the chlorine pool.
Who's to say?

September 11, 2001

earlier that morning
was a wild and terrible passion
and I was cruel I was cruel
though it seemed to be you
and I was wild and you were true
and I was wild and it seemed to be
a cold and terrible passion
and I was lost and you were found
and you found me and I was cold
and we were cold and we were cruel
and I was here and you went there
I was home here and you were working there
I worked here and you worked there
and I was angry at home and you were
in the office there and working in quick anger
and we were cold and I was cruel
and you were fast there in the tower
and working and we were cruel
and cold that morning we lost

Aubade

Between moonlight and sunlight
what lies in shadow is out of our hands.
We rest dreaming
or stand stretching at a window.
An osprey struggles and so does its fish.
A wolf sees beaver, moose, deer.
Her eye is undeceived as ticks move in on her.
We are within the grasp of birdsong enigma
without weather or mortalities.
Our pilgrim stance is lulled.
The sun rises as we dream or gaze.
Later we will say
it must have rained during the night.

Stone is a wad of gum, leaf is a gum wrapper

There were long lists of old things
and new things as yet unlisted
which brings me round to those hang-up phone calls.
Were you crossing things off a list
till you were left with only harass and backpedal?
It was pretty annoying
and I was thinking of getting an unlisted number.
But then you stopped and I was dejected.

Ah yes life does have a way of falling behind
as it catches up. You were gone long before
the phone calls which displayed private caller.

There were lists of synonyms for things like toast, pretend, bachelors.
Bachelors, that could be single guys. Right?
Someone says, I don't think so because
the bachelors are shaving daily
and noting smooth faces. The single guys
are shaving their heads bald.
They want locks but got stuck with tufts.
They say fuck it and shave the works.
The bachelors double-brush and say mother.

As for us, we both wanted to be included
on the right lists. You liked the idea
and I was already there and unconcerned.
Funny how in those days you thought of me as a long-lost twin
though I was way older. These days
it's an open hand coming clean.

Sonnet 7

There is a voice you need to keep at bay
A sound that cracks you like a bone on ice
That frantic pleading stay oh please please stay
I'll talk the dirt and pay your rolling dice.
But you within your playing want no lover
One arm is all you need to scratch and win
Your secret sets no limits under cover
Tonight you think just one more time again.

Blackjack, poker, slots and VLTs
Horses, snooker, craps and odds on dogs
I'm down 'n' dirty, slick-lipped on my knees
Your eyes are tuned to tips from bookmarked blogs.
Two of us are staying as we choose.
Both of us believing as we lose.

Quick question

Speaking of good parenting
I asked her how to be a natural mother. Or she asked me.
It was blowing up a storm and we all knew a south wind brings rain.
At least in that area. You couldn't drink the lake water.
One father added chlorine to a pail of it. The speaker said
boiling would have worked. But it was all after the fact.

No one succeeded at farming and every story was terrible.
I wanted to make pine-needle pincushions to sell. Child's play
but I didn't know how or when to be the mother.
The area was granite rock covered with roots. I was searching
for earth though most girls wanted saddle shoes.

But, and here's where it gets confusing, someone yelled
Listen to this:
I am a rigid angry thing trying to be a mother.
I am a wild shaking thing trying to be a mother.
Don't you know a mother can be a thing of arrogance and narrow mind?

I was leaning on my elbows and staring off.

They said the mother went back into the house-on-fire.
They said the father went too.
They said the parents didn't know the baby was already out and safe.
It grew up as best it could.

Speaking of those days

I was feeling nervous which was puzzling
because nothing had changed.
Girls were still watching girdles
and their mothers' morning struggles
with elastic, talcumed rubber and binderbras.
Mine scrimshawed her way into
a whew as her breasts disappeared.

If you're feeling all nervous
it's never going to work. I was
charading a slow roll of stocking
with jerky gestures standing
astride a middenheap of lingerie. But
we were still deriding ourselves
so there was some laughing.

Did saltimbanques train into change?
Seemed they just ran away
joined up and pretzelled into their pas de deux.
It was puzzling for a tripped-up person
trapped in my own wooden steps.

I was feeling at home in my narcissistic disturbance
knowing nothing had changed.
Girls were still swept up
let down, choosing and discarding
swinging saucy into their surly years.

eau de parfum

A pretty girl was standing
at the foot of the escalator. She was trying
to give away smells. I knew she was going
to corner me because she smiled at my hat.
"No thanks," I said. "I never use that stuff."

"I can't actually spray you," she said, "we're not allowed to
but I can put a squirt on this little blotter
and you can put it up your sleeve or in your underwear."

"No thanks," I said. "I don't like perfume."
"Oh it's not that," she said, "it's eau de
and you don't actually spray your body.
You just shoot a whiff into the air
and walk through it. But I'm not allowed
to do that here. So would you like a little
scented blotter for your personal?"
"No, no thanks," I said.
"Men love this," she said. "Makes them
want to like crazy."

I was getting tired of being polite
and I was feeling hot so I took my hat off.
"Oh," she said. "You want to stick a little blotter in your hat.
What a great idea. I'll have to tell my manager."

"No no," I said. "No blotters. No bottles
of whatever. I'm a grandmother."

I felt compelled to tell her that. My voice was getting
stern and pompous and righteous and prissy.
"Oh," she said. "The old men just love our beautiful products.
They hang around here all the time. You should see."
"Hey," I yelled as I stormed onto the escalator,
"I don't want no ninety-year-old boyfriend."

Echoing down of light

Whatever shadows there are,
it is the one at the moment of attention.
Of seeing here on this morning a small leaf
perched above a larger leaf which holds the shadow
of something smaller than itself
although, in shadow, larger than it is.
This tiny top leaf cast upon
its welcoming sister in this way. How we love
the other children of our parents. Or wish. Or try.
We say, hurrying into speech,
there's lots of time, take it easy
with yesterday, tomorrow and today
and you know what? And then
these pools of shadows
that move like secrets are everything.

I hope it can be my fault for a change

Heading out to spend time with boring people.
Nothing to do with being a force of niceness.

Our tea arrived in that French press contraption
that the server had plunged before steeping.
There was no reversing though I smiled at your efforts.

My self-pity needs replenishing.
It has been draining away, and, as I said,
your compliments are killing me.
You like me. You must be crazy.
I'm way too arrogant for that.
I need more wallowing but the mud level is low.
This being obliging isn't helping any more than chitchat.

Too many bandages with peeling paper and dried-out adhesive.
It's clear more wounds are required around here.
Here's the strop, a tad frayed.
Where's the razor? Superficiality loses things.

So the search is on for a poor-me fill-up.
I need a shot of odd-man-out, some nasty people unlike yourself.
Who just said get lost?

Aubade

At daybreak
I saw you, father,
and we were all of us still in Belfast
intemperate and raging
and my sister had not yet scattered your ashes.
What do roses know about the future?
You were up at dawn fishing
and then we lived here.
I had a baby sister named Fleur.
She came straight from the moon, you said.
I remember her little interferences.
She escaped your insistence
and my attempts at murder.

... don't succeed, try try ...

I attempted to break the channel-surfing habit by systematically limiting the choices. On Saturday the fourth, I was down to two: channel 40 and channel 6. So it was *Ravel's Brain* and *Hockey Night in Canada*.

The doctor sings a report: an accident in a taxi, a blow to the skull. A player is down on the ice. Someone's elbow out of the blue, deliberate and accidental. Whistle, bell and horn in the arena and, would you believe, it is the composer's own music that the surgical records are set to. Is he faking it? He sings like opera, and the player, take a close look, is gripping a stick. Can you do that while comatose? If you bang your head in a taxi, do you lose your music? No, sings the surgeon. It just stays in your brain. You you you are silently agitated. And the hockey player? They carried him off on a stretcher looking dead. Diagnosed concussion. Although later he walked out of the dressing room giving the finger to someone. Ravel looked alive during surgery. No general anaesthetic for brain operations in 1937. Fear of edema, sang the doctor. The hockey guy, Scott somebody, survived. So did Ravel, briefly.

On Sunday the fifth, I gave over the whole day to noting, in my writing, far too many examples of conflation.

A man was walking his dog

Mr. Hyland was walking Quills beside Mimico Creek.
I was quite taken with him and the river
was a raging torrent
so I said, Too much rain.
He said, A likely story.
I knew he meant me so I said, I'm Helen.
He said, You can call me Hill.
I said, The poet I'm reading mentions
a pill of smoke, not that I'm really into rhyme.
He said, Oh Hell
or Oh Helen or O'Hill and I said, You could say
the same thing about drawing, because to get that
compelling awkward placement
of a broken wing at one shadow-filled moment,
it would be like how you must feel
about Quills' bum leg.
Yes, he said, I know a grandchild
who's nimble and quick. Wow, I said, I
saw one with a pie of blackbirds.
And I jumped for joy knowing he still meant me.
None of our business, he said.

Eros errors

The grief of little girls will make them sad and sexy. – Dan Chiasson

Those who lost their sexuality can leave.
Or would if they could.

All girls of the pencilled-on eyebrows
please join the Halter Tops next door. If you
are in the figure-this-out class
sit down if possible.

Those who have their soft parts destroyed
can solidify the remains. Or could
try stone courage.

The bruises are blue
the ulcers are red
this catatonia started in bed
is all in the head
is me playing dead.

Any girls too nervous for arm-in-arm
may proceed single file. But do align yourselves
with those of nodding recognition.

There are spaces left at the back. Any remaining
nulled faces should fill the gaps.

Girls who grieve
can try to leave
the past and stay
and try to play
Hello? No way José.

Those who cut holes in the air and step in
Those who step inside themselves
Those who worry something of themselves in their fingers
Those who stuff their mouths with balled bedsheets
Those who kneel and stroke a holy item

The hope is for a mild disappointment.

One of us is in a Mohawk cemetery

It was another pleasant
afternoon near the river.
There was supper in the slow cooker
and nothing was curled in the storm sewer.
A dog barked Blue Skies two times.
It was a semiotic moment you said. Then you said
actually more 'pataphysical.
And to let myself in I said Meta Meta
Met a man with seven wives. But you
were daydreaming about some girl. I knew
you didn't hear me. Ears are too close to brain.
One newly buried mother leads to another
and ours are eternally elsewhere. Have you ever
loved anything more? Didn't you?
I will warn you: I don't know these mushrooms
and you could wait all summer for someone
to lean into your life.
Or just say Me Me.
I stand corrected: You You.

We see us as we truly behave

Taking him at his word
was a generous gesture.
I could pat myself on the back. But
not really generous because I enjoyed
a superior state, a thoughtless innocence.
Who me? The sweetest person around.

Going to pick up a pizza, return videos, go for a run.
Right you are. And righteous me.
Everything has a value even when
you are boring in your details:
There were slim girls in saris walking along Bloor Street.

Just a comment. Not a hint to lose weight.
What I hear is what you get from me.
No second-guessing face value.

The problem is
assumed naiveté issued once too often
and love breaks away. Real scenery
turns out to be something like background.
Wait, who lied here?

The title of this poem is a line by John Ashbery.

In the beginning was the word

The teacher said, "Choose a word."
I said, "An adverb?"
She said, "Who cares."
I said, "I need direction. A preposition?"
She said, "Geez."
I said, "I like to be proper."

So I chose *with* because I think of myself as a without kind.
Sort of a site for the instruments of longing. Like
dead leaves clinging to a branch. Like Eeyore. Like
stockings riding in rucks round the ankles.
The teacher said, "Get cracking," and I thought of how
I'd shouted at my friend before class.
Being with my friend is now questionable.
"How long is this assignment?" I asked.
"With patience and endurance," she said and I thought about
getting through this so I could return to my math love. But
would I be muddled? Would I remember
how to get over the equal sign?

"OK," she said, "time to wind up,
close it off, summarize your word."
The word was with God.
Where?

Why always me

The teeter-totters have sprung into action
slingshotting toddlers over my way and beyond.
I can only catch so many
with my butterfly net. Luckily
it has a calming effect and
the small fluttering creatures are headed back
for another turn. I feel very responsible
trapped on this footbridge.

It's a cynical Mimico Creek
rounding the bend this morning. I can smell
the nasty mood, stuck as I am on this bridge
of pickpockets and con artists.
The twelve tasks are mine alone:
to shore up the retaining wall
to haul out shopping carts
to smoke out the rats
to sweep off the ladybugs.

And here I am going out on a limb, doing it all.
There's a nuisance philosopher muttering around
getting in the road of my global design.
Speed it up there, droopy eyes.
I'm a sharpshooting broom lady
with the strength of anger and
a foul mouth to boot.

What are those ducks doing
peering up at me like that?

Aubade

At rosy-fingered closing time
I can say Derrida
I can say candida
and I am in Paris with problems
trying to be smart with the tunes
at Le Lapin Agile.
Well it ain't a Chet Baker cover.
Though I'm pretty drunk, that would be Amsterdam
and I'm here with the situation brought from Canada.
Candidiasis. Should've watched the beer.
Sit still. Privilege that. And speech.
Hey Hey. New day. J'ai besoin
d'un médecin.

Living your life

It's not my business but
you do look unfulfilled.
Are you set on holding that empty spot?
I think you should get out more.
Try to fill up on blue skies from now on
nothing but blue skies. Do I see
a little smile? Do I? Do I?
Oops. I agree you don't belong to me
but if you did, is all I'm saying
and I'd never tell you what to do but
I know you are too high strung
to be vocalizing and while we're at it
those pointy diva shoes will lead you
straight into hammer toes. Not good.
Even if you don't get out much.
Hey, just trying to cheer you up is all.
You know what I'm saying. Of course
it's up to you but if I had a voice like yours
I would never be taking singing lessons. That's
likely why you're so depressed. Forget music.
Think golf. The restaurant business. What about
a manager? Or creative writing? How terrific is that?
You'd need a plenitude of foresight.
I'd love it myself. But I'm not you.
You should try to live your own life.
Not depend so much on my advice.

Sketch for April

Richard was planning his Last Supper.
It would be after Stanley Spencer. Something about
bunioned feet and one diner vomiting.

I was trying to make my position known:
a footbridge over Mimico Creek
from where I was planning to catch the Passion Play.

Watch out Richard. You're too close.
They've unscrewed part of the Jesus and
there'll be fireworks for the tomb scene.

Someone yelled Jew. I was planning to say
you never can tell. Someone yelled Liar
and Are You A Girl. No free lunch here.
A child nearby seemed to be wheezing.

Last year when Richard died and I
was planning to go to the funeral
his wife said he's not Jewish
so it can't be on Holy Monday.
Oh, not *this* Richard. That one was from Winnipeg.

It all worked out quite well. Everyone grew into
and I could even catch the odd hey-hosanna from my spot.
Richard changed direction and later I saw my mother.

Touching makes me nervous

My sister, with her children, is travelling north.
My mother has been buried.
My bed and books are moving to a condo.

And where is the question? That moment that asked when?
And someone answered, You'll know.
You'll feel feet under your feet.

But I remembered a bride with a groom on a big cake
and that looked correct.
If you blame anything a bell rings and a light flashes.
In this way, you mistakenly think you're right.

The covenant is between your memory and your ruminations.

You and I got married.
Not you with me on the journey.
You with me, was fanciful
was seeming.

The work of mourning

Heartening to see all these widows out in the air.
Out and about finally, or too soon.
I can't tell which. I am one.

The seas are rough or calm and the older ones
won't remember. The younger ones won't either eventually.

"The thing to remember is there is money to be made in keratin.
Yes ladies, you can take both
the manicure and the investment seminar." I can't decide.

Those in the know speak of pitting,
dull ridges, vertical faults, fungal infections, white spots.

Arresting to see all these women forcibly cheerful,
growing into the maiden aunts they could have been.

"Keratin can stand on its own or profit from veneers.
A fortune if we could replicate the Cremonese varnish.
We need someone to think in widdershins."

What is this? This quick Cruise to Recovery.
Those in the know speak of staying the course,
diversifying, tweaking, risk tolerance, balanced portfolios.

I'm pretty sure I'm starboard and doing my best
watching the growing pile of cuttings and parings.

He would've loved this blatant irony. Where is he
now that I have money and a death certificate?

"Come ladies, rough seas ahead" and we're all in the red
polish line-up as everything careens seaward
all bottles are buys.

On the brink, beyond itself,
grief allows nothing.

October

This is not the time to keep quiet
to sew or pore over figures.
This is a time for large gestures
pitched sweaters and flung leaves.
The temperature climbs and slides
in weeks of clomping and tramping.
There's no tiptoeing here.
Muscled wind boots the cheering and waving.
Arms are open. Mounds let off steam.
Clear out the sky and show me Pegasus.

Bring it on home to me

Everyone was arguing.
She said I was cheating
which was true but
I said I wasn't even playing
which was true until the tall guy said
You're either in or out make up your mind
which I had been trying to do all along.
Some of them said that's an insane decision
and wandered off. I did my usual.

One of the paler performers shouted
Am I black enough?
I've shaved off all my mother-given hair.
Am I a brother? A woman sang
Black man cheat. Black man lie.
Black man make de woman cry.
And white I said to myself.

It was a story of how we weren't.
You weren't supposed to say lover
and make everyone up in arms.
I wasn't expected to do much. A lot
of them loved the limelight and
noticed nothing. We weren't
all that particular and no one
was completely caught out.
It came. It went. Small revisions
and see-through alibis.
I still say we knew what we were doing.

My new job

He said, Fire the nurse, she steals paper howls.
OK, I said, But I think you mean towels.
No no, he said, I meant chef. Fire that guy, he burns things.
Who hired you anyway?

I could see he was pressed for patience
and I too was feeling night clouds
so when he shouted,
Ground is something more than sand and gravel you know,
I stuck out all my knives and forked tongues.
Pluck rainbows, I said.
Weep off.

!!!!!

When the wild things are
on a tear
bells peal, canons fire.
They pull out all stops and
everything is done glancingly.

The problem with science is it's too long.
You want the answer.
Was loving life ever up there?

It's only an experiment if it can fail.
If it fails, it was only an experiment.
Where's the frenergy in that?

More and more lightning every year.
That patch of dry grass is
shaped like a fire hydrant. Help!
Is that weed growing wild in there?
Talk about your glissandi and clusters,
the problem with music is it's too slow.
Zut alors, speed up that Ravel, will you!

Are you hungry? Congratulations!
I'm in the midst of I forget what.
No doubt it was sensational, a superabundance.
Put on the flak vest and helmet.
Double your bet or fold. Extra deck
hidden in the ... Whooee
what a ride, this full-tilt posturing!

Full circle

He said,
You don't want to buy this place. There's nothing here.
He looked up at clouds and said, See what I mean?

It was very dark
and after I bought it
whenever I walked to the end
I could examine
what had stuck to my boots. I could see
what he thought he'd meant.

The need is to stay out of earshot of crackpots.
Though I sneak in humiliated, I am a conscientious coward.
Everything gets inventoried: 4 miscarriages; 2 ectopics.

I wear nice clothes and lipstick
to walk to the end of the moist green, stamp down
any clumps that have arisen.

What is buried here was unable to find a way:
a fetus returned from the lab, a ginger cat
caught in traffic, a wedding ring.

If it starts out damp, dark and inviting
you're pretty sure you have a chance, and thus
the elf face, chubby legs, stuttering chin of a newborn.

Aubade

At dawn
one toothache
and a couple of disappointing mutual funds
are sufficient collaboration
to spoil the sunrise
and I wonder
why I ever was impressed
with that principal clarinetist
who told me that, in 1946, more doctors
smoked Camels than any other cigarette.
Ahem. Phlegm at 6 a.m. Could be throat cancer
or an abscess
and expensive root canal job.

Departure Lounge

What were you telling him about me? I saw you talking to him.
What were you saying? You were over there talking. I saw you say me.

About your audience size, your emerging markets and poets,
your low overhead, bangs and bangles, your posture and grammar.

Did you say, "*This here's Miss Bonnie Parker.
We rob banks.*"

I said second of all a pistol does not automatically
go off by being dropped on the floor.

OK I heard you mention Christmas.
Did you say it still works in prison?

I said jail's nothing to them. They're in 'n' out. "*I'm no loverboy.*"
And both of your mothers call you Bertie.

Behind my back? Outside my window?
In the dark? All the way to the escape clause?

You're a real trial and error, you are. I said
you were spotted making out in Montreal and Moncton.

That's great. Saves me having to tell the details.
Thanks so much. Let me give you a hug.

Lipogram Award (no E allowed)

Its omission constant, by my calculation, is high.
So writing this limit? Playwork. Go for it.

I bring a tray of drinks. Martinis and so on.
You say fuckit, I'm stuck.

Too dry, that's all. Chinup
girl. Who's at your door? A man

from Porlock. Yeah right. Any irony
will do. Old stalling tactic. Nothing doing.

Grasp this constraint and grab a schnapps. No
naps till closing hour. I want

you to win this thing.
I could do it. Look,

"and drunk blah-blah milk of blah-blah."
You can put that in. It's fair.

Kubla Khan. Ku Klux Klan. Don't act so picky.
Why's your laptop hiding in that hood?

I know you
usually court inspiration. But no not now.

Push particulars. Try using D minor.
Think Oulipo stuff. All OK.

Good job, scriptor.
Missing it still is going going

Short history of her, once and for all

She was an only child.
In kindergarten got a sister.

It was your regular sweet 'n' sours:
ballet, strappings, birding.

Hard to say about family ways.
Or the scalding, drowning, smothering attempts.

With sisters pitted against each other,
everyone had to yell or shutup.

And grow up we did, left and right,
stuck in eating and drinking.

Mother loved a grate fire in memory.
Dad undercover. Things not

all hunky-dory yet. No question.
For now no more questions for once.

Aubade

Sunrise
and the most reliable thing
is the way you lose all courage.
It slips off in a graceful fall
that starts at 3 a.m.
By dawn you are weightless
in your gluttony of fear.
Suspicious of past success
and all compliments
you are Yeats' paltry thing
a mess of wine and junkfood
crouching with binoculars
to spot coyotes
moving cityward.

In regard to Yes

A truth about Yes lies in repetition.
The Molly Bloom thing.
Even singular the possibility lies in a preceding question.
So the answer is the second occurrence.
Waking to warm sun, I shout YES.
Have I never done that before?
Again and again?

A truth about Yes lies in reassurance.
I told you, YES. How many times do I need to say it?
Well, when did you start?
You and I are both missing out here.
It's not a bad thing to say it again tomorrow.
That way, you can't excuse yourself.
Can't squirm out of it.
I'm as good as my word, is a promise to remember.

Do you take him to be your that? I do.
Not Yes. The personal answer
lets in the future changed minds.
No is not the undoing of Yes.

But also in repetitions, the vocable reality.
Yes,yes,yes, I know. So what else is new?
Finally.

Yes, I said. I can write my life in anecdotal lyrics.
But next winter? Will I be able to lift Yes with each shovelful of snow?
After such puffery?

Speaking of Yes, the strongest case would be amen.

December

Excerpt: On the Sunday after Christmas, spent time in examination of myself in the mirror.

Flesh becoming Word

A poem could say
the aging genitals as they are:
withered floppy labia; puckered clitoral shawl;
long gaping fissure. All intruded upon by
sparse, coarse, white hairs.
In the midst of this, an exuding other than desire.

A painting would seem less repulsive,
wouldn't contain the imagined reality words give.
The nasty odour implied wouldn't occur.
One's eyes would be held fascinated
by something. Something productive.

Excerpt: K's birthday on the 29th. After dinner, talk with her about Egon Schiele's pictures. She said they are worse than pornography because with porn there is a superficial level of beauty. But Schiele gives us bony, awkward geeks masturbating. No one wants to look at that. She said.

Typeset in Boldface Pandora, title boxed

Not a bad way to start the afternoon
whistling, waiting, wanting
to think reverse and reserve
enough so they flow to each other
in a simple way so to say as:
turn back, hold back, withhold.

We agreed
to meet at the sale table by the cash
where I was just about to understand
landscape as mood and get a grip
but I lost it in the crying mother
of a lost child. She was sobbing
that she felt so guilty. I asked
what she was doing. Sobbing, she said.
I think you need more guilt, I said.

Waiting in other days we helped fetch
bier and pall from the graveyard's stonehouse.
School was closed. No whistling.
Walking children followed the little dead one.

Waiting in Pythagorean reverie
at the 31 flavours 2-for-1 triple scoops
I was just about to want a five-year secrecy.
But the afternoon was closing and would yield
to relative silence or outright silencing.

The shadow life

Nimble and quick
we are the costume winners
rapid-fire name-changers
hat-switching masters
of the postures of trades.

No procrastinations
all eyes and ears
focus champions
spewing stories everyone falls for.

We know what we need
and you are it, pal.

We never yawn on the job
snap at the staff
trip on a mat.

And if you are left
holding the empty
bag, wallet, promise,
well
it feels like your fault.

And hey,
if you're cured of your seizures
does it matter today
if the surgeon's on call or in jail?

How many times do I have to

Strips of indifference fresh from the paper shredder.
Things that seemed important at the time.
The way a poignant moment can go up in smoke
and, as he said, into the corners of the evening.

No, no, not Pound. The other one who went to England.
Who am I thinking of? You know who I mean.

It becomes a fault for not being a mind reader.
A momentary irritation that branches off into wisps
or curlicues that remind us of dollar signs.
I'd been trying all morning to remember that sign
for the British pound. Something like an L.

It's true I am partially greedy. Which means
I'm mostly too lazy to shoplift or steal
a swung vase from the shelf in this gallery.
It never works out anyway. Like the time I got the TV stand
into the van but we didn't have a place to live.
You can't keep everything in mind.

So where were we? Oh yes, Scotland.
No, no, that spot was near Belfast.
But we did use the same currency. At least you did.
I'd lost my wallet. Couldn't find my pocket.

Zoobird theatre

The language of birds is not zoobird language.
Here they prefer to be prompted in Latin.
They say *In my zoo* and *To you I am Pavo*.
No one says *But you might try*
even with two sides to the glass. Two years ago
it was the same and so on.

A zoobird went to a store and my sister
brought it home in its house for which she got
a mother tongue lashing. *Get that thing out of here.*
In the midst, the zoobird flew off into our trees.
My sister yelled the name she gave it. Why
did it come back?

Not a dry eye in the house. This is how they avoid war.
Everything enters and exits. A stone-dry throat,
a braked red eye, wings oil-spilled or pizza-cheese globbed.

I listen to the zoobirds and see how it unfolds.
We take turns all at once. What's your favourite part?
The curtain went up.
A language tough strutted. I didn't catch the ending.

Perpetual cleanup

Fly you, wildbird
half eaten by the smog.
All sheets to the wind. Oh oh
is it laundry day? These perversions
are so mainstream since we lost count.
I used to say please
before you exposed me.
In your dreams, you said.
Now it's all lost
in the bed linen. We wake up
to the sounds of development.
Is that Mimico Creek
in the washing machine? If you roll over
you're out of the dream and your anger
can really take shape. Sorry,
I meant passion.

Don't worry Frizzhead if the poetry thing don't work out I'll buy you a hairdressing place

Good title, eh.
Now I have to write the poem.
I, has a scratched throat
and a mystery stuck to the palate.
Where's the edgewise word?
Silver apples aren't the moon.
Nothing seems to be slouching to be born.
An aged man, a tattered coat
are just that. Go elsewhere.
If a bare branch in winter is a line
snow there is line upon line.
But to do that in that way.

I applied the straightening solution.
I waited a long time.
I applied the neutralizer
and wound in large rollers.
I could never predict the outcome:
beautiful lines that broke at their roots
wavy lines that shone from product content
new highlights by chemical chance.
How could you do that?
I needed a threshold in that way.
Like small talk, you could say.
I mean power lines, not meaning.

Can I have a word with you?
Did we have words?

He has a book on the wall

Hey, I'm like that too.
Drawing a face on everything.
A face with teeth. Freddie Mercury's teeth.
Acoustic mark.

Right now I'm not trying to sing.
It just comes out like that.
Humming over every errand
so you avoid the wholehearted effort
and sidestep to now and lose
yourself in never wanting to really know.

I keep a low profile everywhere
like the horizon or erotica
which isn't anything else
or a symbol of anything.
This comes easy as kindness becoming a nuisance.

If the intention is to be always
nodding and agreeing
how does graceful form infuse anger?
As in: How do I take care of you now that you're gone?

He too has the autodidact's arrogance.
That book is Mimico Creek music
of which we could've been the Paul Simon
instead of these one-note ducks.
Threnody for the quacks.

Hotel Everlasting

Many things about the place are puzzling.
The man behind the counter answers your queries
      (is there a roof garden
        what's that sign mean
        is the money safe)
by offering his profile
which is fine I guess. He's handsome enough.
The woman behind the roller cart
could be in love but
I think I'm wrong here. Nobody
looks at her twice and she's parked
at a very unlucky number. Rolls and towels
seem to have slowed her down
usurped her storage space
and her sparkle.
Well we all change, get tired
but you'd think they could delve a bit. After all
we did pre-book the works including
ferry ride, gulls, slapping sounds, arms around waists,
the usual last ditch attempt to salvage eros.

And so we check in
at these places where treats on the dresser
and small soaps on the sink remind us to be happy.
What's that? you yell from the shower
as hard candies ping the plastic curtain.
Getting us in the mood, I say. You know
like mini-bars, room service, piles of pillows.
Everything is promised, if we aim ourselves
at some near, as yet unattainable, mark.

Precursors

The look of a word
is also a meaning
It looks staringly
intention abdicates
and you set it down
Woods, he wrote
lovely, dark etc.
Ah yes
I find that won't do
I need to
mind the hidden
seeing with a touch of sense
One from the other
all things touch so they are
in poem
Voice formed from life
not personal property
Whose woods these
itinerantly
and with easement
No anxiety influence
Grand march of saturations
she writes
unquoted
enthusiastic thanks

Lines upon line

How many lines begin with at the end

Did the line determine how she filled it

The last line on the last page is no example

There was one complaint that the line is obscene or obscure

There is one complete passage that takes nine lines

Five lines are back to front and the other four ellipsed

The spread of a line has the look of a meaning

The look of a line is casual announcing and omitting connectives

A line is thin
A thin bare line can a lot
It is able and capable of ample
It is once or every fourth

In a first skimming she grasped a few felicitous lines

A line that supposedly explains what isn't grasped

From line to line how it speaks

O you of the playful animating line of manic mocking monologue

Forbidding assignment rising from any line

Please take your thoughts is the shortest line and will come at the end

Acknowledgements

Some of these poems have appeared in the following publications:
*The Antigonish Review, The Best Canadian Poetry in English 2008,
CV2, The Dalhousie Review, The Fiddlehead, Grain, The Malahat
Review, The New Quarterly, Prairie Fire, PRISM international,
The Windsor Review.*

I am grateful for the support of the Toronto Arts Council and
the Ontario Arts Council.

Heather Cadsby was born in Belleville Ontario and moved to Toronto at a young age. She obtained a B.A. degree from McMaster University and taught elementary school for a number of years. In the 1980s she helped organize poetry readings at the Axle-Tree Coffee House in Toronto. Recently she has served as a director of the Art Bar Poetry Series. *Could be* is her fourth book of poetry.